W9-CBM-911

TODAY'S NFL
12 REASONS FANS FOLLOW THE GAME

by Drew Silverman

12 STORY LIBRARY

www.12StoryLibrary.com

Copyright © 2016 by Peterson Publishing Company, North Mankato, MN 56003. All rights reserved. No part of this book may be reproduced or utilized in any form or by any means without written permission from the publisher.

12-Story Library is an imprint of Peterson Publishing Company and Press Room Editions.

Produced for 12-Story Library by Red Line Editorial

Photographs ©: Julio Cortez/AP Images, cover, 1, 6; Nam Y. Huh/AP Images, 4, 9, 29; Paul Spinelli/AP Images, 5, 14; Gene J. Puskar/AP Images, 8, 28; Charlie Riedel/AP Images, 10; Stephen Chernin/AP Images, 12; Dean Bertoncelj/Shutterstock Images, 15; Robert Pernell/ Shutterstock Images, 16; Ken Durden/Shutterstock Images, 17; David Stluka/AP Images, 18; Rick Osentoski/AP Images, 20; Brian Ach/NFL Fantasy Draft Week: Direct TV Party/AP Images, 22; David J. Phillip/AP Images, 25, 26

ISBN
987-1-63235-158-6 (hardcover)
978-1-63235-198-2 (paperback)
978-1-62143-250-0 (hosted ebook)

Library of Congress Control Number: 2015934303

Printed in the United States of America
Mankato, MN
June, 2015

Go beyond the book. Get free, up-to-date content on this topic at 12StoryLibrary.com.

TABLE OF CONTENTS

QUARTERBACKS TAKE OVER THE NFL

There has never been a better time to be a quarterback in the National Football League (NFL). Of course, quarterbacks have always been important. They lead a team's offense. They touch the ball on every play. But the NFL has made quarterbacks even more important.

Football began as a running game. The first quarterbacks were not even allowed to throw forward passes. However, NFL teams began passing more and more. Fans loved it. So the league made it easier to pass. Rule changes protected quarterbacks and gave receivers more room to make plays. Today's rulebook basically encourages quarterbacks to pass.

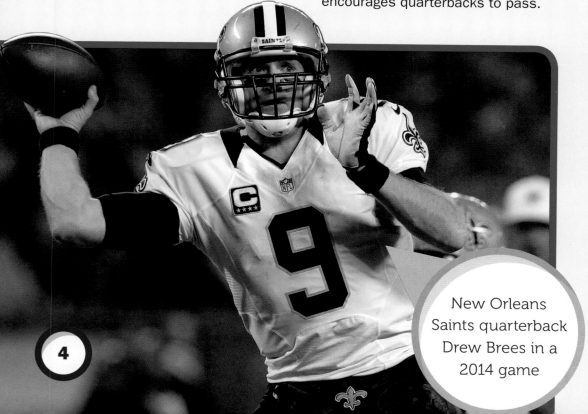

New Orleans Saints quarterback Drew Brees in a 2014 game

Having a good quarterback is essential these days. Just ask the New England Patriots. Tom Brady led that team to its fourth Super Bowl win in February 2015. The Denver Broncos' Peyton Manning has set dozens of passing records. Green Bay Packers quarterback Aaron Rodgers and New Orleans Saints quarterback Drew Brees are expert passers, too. And Seattle Seahawks quarterback Russell Wilson has another weapon. When there are no open receivers, he can take off and run down the field himself.

Quarterbacks dominate the league's major awards. Meanwhile, the Super Bowl almost always features star quarterbacks. It's no surprise so many teams pick quarterbacks in the first round of the NFL Draft each year.

"It's clear that you are witnessing some of the greatest quarterbacks to ever play the game out there right now," said Brees. Yet he added, "Maybe our best is yet to come."

New England Patriots quarterback Tom Brady won his third Super Bowl MVP Award in February 2015.

7

Seasons in which a quarterback won the NFL Most Valuable Player (MVP) Award from 2007 to 2014.

- In 18 NFL Drafts from 1998 to 2015, the first pick was a quarterback 13 times.
- The forward pass was illegal in organized football until 1906.

5

AMAZING ATHLETES LIGHT UP THE FIELD

Odell Beckham Jr. amazed fans on November 23, 2014. The New York Giants' wide receiver ran toward the end zone. A long pass sailed his way. But Beckham got tangled up with the defender. The pass was high. But Beckham went higher. He stretched his body high into the air and grabbed the ball with one hand. Touchdown!

NFL players are some of the best athletes in the world. Every position requires a different skill set. But today's players have few

The Giants' Odell Beckham Jr. makes an amazing touchdown catch against the Dallas Cowboys in 2014.

4.24

Seconds in which running back Chris Johnson ran the 40-yard dash at the 2008 combine. That was a record.

- In 1999, Justin Ernest set a new combine record by doing 51 reps on the bench press.
- Gerald Sensabaugh holds the combine record for the vertical jump. He leaped 46 inches (117 cm) in 2005.

STARS IN OTHER SPORTS

Several NFL players have starred in other sports as well. Tight ends Jimmy Graham and Antonio Gates were college basketball players. Quarterbacks Tom Brady, Russell Wilson, and Colin Kaepernick were all chosen in the Major League Baseball draft. Other football players have competed in track and field in the Olympics. Among them are Lawrence Okoye and Marquise Goodwin.

weaknesses. Skill position players are often lightning fast. Some can leap high into the air. Even most linemen are great athletes. They are big and strong. But they also must be very quick and nimble, too.

Fans can see these amazing athletes every Sunday. That athleticism is measured each February at the NFL Scouting Combine. Players likely to be drafted show off their tools there. They run the 40-yard dash to demonstrate their speed. They do a shuttle run to show their agility. They bench press 225 pounds (102 kg) as many times as possible to show their strength.

Of course, players need to be skilled to succeed in the NFL. But great athleticism doesn't hurt. Each year, players rise and fall in the NFL Draft based on their performances at the combine.

RIVALRIES RILE UP RABID FANS

The roots of the NFL date back to 1920. Some teams have been playing each other nearly that long. The Green Bay Packers and Chicago Bears have played in the same division since 1933. The New York Giants and the Philadelphia Eagles have been grouped together since then, too. Only in 1967 and 1969 were they apart. It's no surprise that these teams have developed fierce rivalries over the years.

But NFL rivals don't have to be old. The Baltimore Ravens only began playing in 1996. They quickly developed a rivalry with the Pittsburgh Steelers.

The Pittsburgh Steelers' James Harrison sacks Baltimore Ravens quarterback Joe Flacco in 2011.

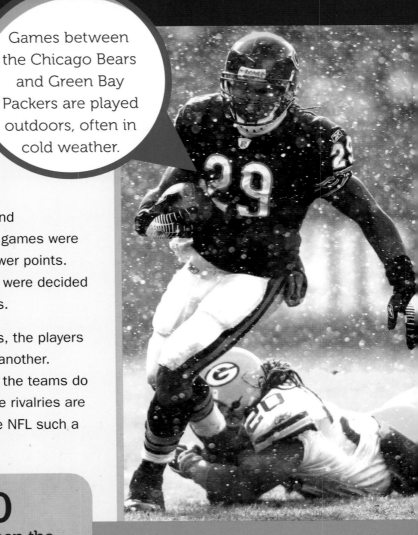

Games between the Chicago Bears and Green Bay Packers are played outdoors, often in cold weather.

Both teams played punishing styles of football. They played 20 times between 2005 and 2013. Fifteen of those games were decided by seven or fewer points. Twelve of those games were decided by three or fewer points.

With some NFL rivalries, the players simply do not like one another. Oftentimes the fans of the teams do not get along. Yet these rivalries are part of what makes the NFL such a great league.

190

Games between the Chicago Bears and Green Bay Packers between 1921 and 2014.

- NFL teams play the other teams in their division twice each year.
- The NFL often schedules rival teams for its national TV broadcasts.

HE SAID IT

"The rivalry is the thing. The Green Bay–Chicago series hasn't become famous because of any particular player, or coaches, or any era's team. . . . The good players come and go. The rivalry goes on."
—Legendary Bears coach George Halas in 1962

THE SUPER BOWL BECOMES SUPER BIG

No US sporting event is bigger than the Super Bowl. It has been the NFL's championship game since the 1966 season. Super Bowl Sunday has since grown to become an unofficial national holiday.

Today's Super Bowl has two weeks of buildup. That gives the conference champions more time to prepare. It also means more media coverage. More than 5,500 media members covered Super Bowl XLIX after the

A fan looks over the field before Super Bowl XLIII in February 2009.

6

Super Bowl wins for the Pittsburgh Steelers. No team has won more.

- The six highest-rated TV shows in US history are Super Bowls.
- Super Bowl halftime shows feature some of the world's most famous musicians.
- Halftime performers have included Beyoncé, Katy Perry, Prince, and Paul McCartney.

PRICEY TICKETS

Most NFL stadiums hold approximately 70,000 fans. Getting a ticket to the Super Bowl can be expensive, though. Super Bowl XLVIII was after the 2013 season. Tickets cost between $800–$1,900. Many fans resold their tickets for much higher prices.

2014 season. Journalists came from all over the world to report about the big game.

The stadium is always sold out. Most fans watch the game on TV. And the Super Bowl is usually the most-watched TV show in the United States each year. A record 114.5 million Americans watched Super Bowl XLIX. That huge audience attracts a lot of advertisers. Companies paid approximately

$4.5 million for a 30-second commercial during the game. With such a high price, companies often make special commercials. Some fans tune in just to watch them.

Most people tune in for the game, though. It is often exciting. Super Bowl XXXIV was held after the 1999 season. The St. Louis Rams won on the final play. The New England Patriots played in six Super Bowls from the 2001 to 2014 seasons. All were decided by four points or fewer.

THE NFL DRAFT HITS THE BIG TIME

Cam Newton poses with NFL commissioner Roger Goodell at the 2011 draft. The Carolina Panthers picked Newton first overall.

32 million

Viewers who watched the first round of the 2014 NFL Draft on TV. That set a record.

- The first NFL Draft was held in 1936.
- The draft was first televised in 1980.

THINK ABOUT IT

Quarterback Russell Wilson fell to the third round of the 2012 draft. That means every NFL team passed on him at least once. Yet he led the Seattle Seahawks to a Super Bowl victory in only his second season. Why do you think it's so hard to predict if a player will be a superstar?

Fans can't seem to get enough of the NFL. Not convinced? Look no further than the NFL Draft. That event is held each spring. Teams take turns picking former college players. Today's draft is seven rounds. Approximately 250 players are chosen. And fans can watch the three-day event live on three different channels.

For fans, the draft is about hope. The draft order is based on the previous season's standings. The team that finished with the worst record owns the first pick in each round. With so many good college players available, one smart pick can be the difference between a winning and losing season.

The draft's first round is the most popular. Players selected in that round are expected to become stars. Many are already famous from their college careers. Fans read news about the draft all year. Experts create mock drafts months in advance. Mock drafts predict which players the teams will pick.

Nobody knows for sure how a player will perform in the NFL, though. The Indianapolis Colts had the first overall pick in 1998 and 2012. They selected Peyton Manning and Andrew Luck in those drafts. Both became superstar quarterbacks. Meanwhile, Tom Brady won his fourth Super Bowl after the 2014 season. Yet he was the 199th overall pick in 2000.

13

DIEHARD FANS CREATE AN AWESOME ATMOSPHERE

Pittsburgh Steelers fans wave their "Terrible Towels." Buffalo Bills and Green Bay Packers fans brave freezing temperatures at late-season home games. Seattle Seahawks fans are so loud they are known as "The 12th Man." Players say their support makes it feel as though the

Oakland Raiders fans cheer on their team in costumes.

Seahawks have 12 players on the field.

NFL fans are passionate and loyal. They create home-field advantages that really show. The Seahawks went 26–2 at home from 2012 to 2014. That included four playoff wins. Oakland Raiders fans didn't have as much to cheer for. Their

Pittsburgh Steelers fans wave "Terrible Towels."

team made the Super Bowl after the 2002 season. Then it went more than a decade without making the playoffs. Yet diehard fans continued to show up wearing face paint and crazy costumes. The intimidating group is known as "The Black Hole."

Fans don't have to act wild to make a difference, though. They just have to show up. And they always do. An amazing 17.3 million fans supported their teams at games in 2013.

142.2

Decibels recorded at a 2014 Kansas City Chiefs game. That is louder than a jet takeoff and an NFL record.

- Seattle Seahawks fans held the previous noise record when they reached 137.6 decibels at a 2013 game.
- Chiefs fans are known for tailgating before games.
- A marching band played at Baltimore Colts games until the team left in 1984. The band came back when the Ravens moved to Baltimore in 1996.

THINK ABOUT IT

Name a situation within a football game when loud fans could affect the play on the field. Explain how their cheers would make a difference.

STUNNING STADIUMS SHOWCASE THE STARS

Soldier Field opened on the banks of Lake Michigan in 1924. The Chicago Bears started playing there in 1971. Fans love Soldier Field for its history. Many great Bears teams took the field on cold fall days there. Yet today's fans crave more than history. So in 2003, Soldier Field was renovated. It's one of many amazing stadiums in today's NFL.

The Dallas Cowboys' AT&T Stadium is massive. More than 100,000 fans can attend games. A huge video scoreboard makes sure they catch all the action. It is more than 50 yards long.

Heinz Field in Pittsburgh

The scoreboard at AT&T Stadium is half as long as the field.

Many technology companies are based around San Francisco. So when the 49ers opened Levi's Stadium in 2014, they made it the league's most tech-savvy stadium. The Arizona Cardinals have a unique home field. The grass can be rolled outside so it can grow in the sunlight. Then it's rolled back inside University of Phoenix Stadium for games. The Jacksonville Jaguars have a swimming pool at EverBank Field.

Many modern NFL stadiums have roofs. Some of those roofs can open up to the elements. Either way, the roofs make late-season games more comfortable for fans. Cold-weather cities Detroit and Minneapolis have even hosted Super Bowls in covered stadiums.

$1.6 billion

Cost to build MetLife Stadium in New Jersey. The New York Giants and Jets' home was the NFL's most expensive.

- The two teams in New York—the Giants and Jets—share the NFL's largest stadium. It seats more than 82,000 fans.
- Twenty-two new NFL stadiums opened between 1992–2014.

TRADITIONS MAKE SUNDAYS COME ALIVE

The clock counted down to zero. That's when the Seattle Seahawks players made their move. They grabbed a giant orange cooler. They sneaked up to coach Pete Carroll. Then they soaked him with Gatorade.

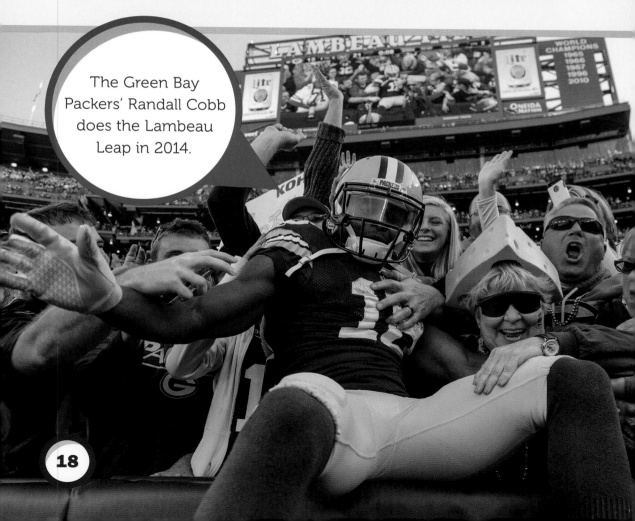

The Green Bay Packers' Randall Cobb does the Lambeau Leap in 2014.

It's a tradition most coaches don't seem to mind. After all, it usually occurs after a big win. In this case, it was the Seahawks' win in Super Bowl XLVIII in February 2014.

The NFL is built on traditions. Each team has its own traditions. In Green Bay, Packers players do the Lambeau Leap after touchdowns. That's when they jump into the crowd. In Minnesota, Vikings fans sing along to "Skol Vikings." In New England, the End Zone Militia shoots muskets after every Patriots score. A cannon shoots off after Tampa Bay Buccaneers touchdowns. Meanwhile, New York Jets fans love to chant "J-E-T-S! Jets! Jets! Jets!"

Many fans also create their own traditions at home. Most NFL games are on Sundays. That allows fans to plan their day around the games. Sometimes that means waking up early and tailgating. Or other fans might prefer to order a pizza and find a comfortable spot on the couch. There's really no wrong way to watch an NFL game. And that's a big reason why fans keep coming back for more.

3
Games played each year on Thanksgiving.

- The Detroit Lions have hosted a Thanksgiving game every year since 1934.
- The Dallas Cowboys began their traditional Thanksgiving home game in 1966.
- A third game rotates between different cities.

RAISING AWARENESS

NFL games in October feature a lot of pink. Many players use pink gloves, wristbands, and even shoes. There are pink logos on the footballs. Pink ribbons can be found all around the stadiums. The NFL began this tradition to raise awareness of breast cancer. Pink represents that cause.

TV BRINGS FANS INTO THE GAMES

NFL stadiums can hold tens of thousands of people. If fans can't watch a game in person, the NFL wants to make sure they watch it on TV or other devices. The league makes sure its broadcasts are top-notch. And new features are constantly added to improve the experience.

A Skycam goes right over the field to bring fans into the action.

3

NFL games that are broadcast nationally each week. They are on Thursday, Sunday, and Monday nights.

- The NFL Network launched in 2003 to give fans 24/7 access to the league.
- Fans can buy a TV package that allows them to watch every NFL game each season.

NFL REDZONE

The NFL introduced the NFL RedZone channel in 2009. This channel bounces from game to game across the country. It focuses on games where one team is within 20 yards of the end zone. This area is called the red zone. The channel allows fans to watch important plays across every game. It also shows highlights of earlier action.

The NFL first began using instant replay in 1986. Today it is an important part of each game. Dozens of cameras film the action. Those camera angles give fans a great view of the game. They also help officials make sure they get calls correct. If a team disagrees with a call on the field, it can challenge the call using instant replay.

In 1998, TV viewers started noticing a new line on the field. The yellow line showed where a team had to get for a first down. Today similar lines show the line of scrimmage and field goal range.

Other technology helps TV viewers feel as if they are in the stadium. High-definition TV became the norm in the early 2000s. Watching sports was never better. The action was clearer on TV than ever before. Meanwhile, microphones on the field capture the sounds of the game.

FANTASY FOOTBALL TAKES OVER

NFL fans don't just cheer on their favorite NFL teams these days. They cheer on their favorite fantasy football teams, too.

Fantasy football is a game in which players make their own teams using real NFL players. The "owners" get points based on how the NFL players

DIRECTV FANTASY FOOTBALL DRAFT

TEAM		ROUND 1		ROUND 2		ROUND 3	ROUND 4	ROUND 5	ROUND 6
STARCOM	RB	A Peterson	QB	A Rodgers	WR	D Thomas			
GROUP M	RB	A Foster	TE	J Graham	WR	L Fitzgerald			
TARGETCAST	RB	D Martin	RB	M Forte	QB	P Manning			
MILLERCOORS	RB	J Charles	WR	J Jones (ATL)	WR	R Cobb			
OPTIMUM SPORTS	RB	L McCoy	WR	B Marshall	QB	T Brady			
VERSACE VERSACE	RB	R Rice	WR	A Green	RB	S Ridley			
UNIVERSAL MCCANN	WR	C Johnson (DET)	RB	C Johnson (TEN)	WR	A Johnson			
OMD	RB	C Spiller	QB	D Brees	WR	V Jackson			
DIGITAS	RB	M Lynch	RB	A Morris	WR	D Bowe			
MAGNA	RB	T Richardson	WR	D Bryant					

A giant fantasy football draft board

perform in their games. People have been playing fantasy football for years. The games exploded in popularity in the late 1990s, though. That's because the Internet made it much easier to play. In 2013, more than 33 million people played fantasy football.

There are many types of fantasy football leagues. Head-to-head leagues are very popular. That's when two fantasy teams compete against each other each week. Roto leagues last all season. The team with the most points at the end wins. No matter what format, most leagues start with a draft. That's when fantasy team owners pick real players. The owners then decide which players to use each week. They can also trade players with other teams.

Many companies offer fantasy football. Websites, TV shows, podcasts, and apps give fantasy advice. The game's popularity has even changed how people watch real games. The NFL RedZone Channel focuses only on the big plays.

$13.4 billion

Estimated money that businesses lose each year because employees spend time managing their fantasy football teams at work.

- Fantasy owners often pick quirky or unique team names.
- Most leagues hold a draft before every season. In keeper leagues, owners hold onto their players from year to year.

THINK ABOUT IT

The San Francisco 49ers' stadium has a fantasy football lounge. Fans can hang out there and focus on their fantasy teams. Do you think this makes the overall fan experience better or worse? Explain why.

FANS EXPECT THE UNEXPECTED

"Any given Sunday." That's a popular saying in football. It means that anything can happen in any NFL game. That motto is definitely true in today's NFL. No lead is ever safe. No win is ever guaranteed.

The Oakland Raiders had lost their first 10 games in 2014. Meanwhile, the Kansas City Chiefs started 7–3. Yet when they met in Week 12, the Raiders won 24–20. One week later, the New York Giants led the Jacksonville Jaguars 21–0. Then Jacksonville came back to win 25–24. The San Diego Chargers had their own amazing comeback that day. They trailed the Baltimore Ravens 30–20. Less than four minutes remained. Yet the Chargers came back to win 34–33 in the final seconds. Any given Sunday.

Even the playoffs are unpredictable. The 2007 New England Patriots didn't lose a game all season. Meanwhile, the Giants had barely made the playoffs. Yet in Super Bowl XLII, the Giants shocked the Patriots with a 17–14 win. With amazing comebacks and upsets almost every week, it's no wonder fans keep tuning in.

32

Points by which the Buffalo Bills trailed the Houston Oilers in a January 1993 playoff game. Buffalo came back to win.

- NFL rules help keep the league competitive.
- The NFL Draft makes sure the worst teams get the first choice for new players.
- Winning teams have harder schedules the next season. Losing teams have easier ones.

The New York Giants' Michael Strahan celebrates after their upset win in Super Bowl XLII.

THE NFL IS EVERYWHERE

NFL teams play games from September to February. Even in the offseason, though, the NFL never stops. The league makes sure it is constantly in the news.

As soon as the Super Bowl ends, fans start thinking about the NFL Draft. The scouting combine is a few weeks after the Super Bowl. It gives fans a look at the top players.

NFL fans get pumped up before a game at Wembley Stadium in England.

3

NFL games held each year in London, England, beginning in 2014.

- The NFL is trying to gain popularity outside the United States.
- The league is considering adding a team in London.

18 GAMES?

NFL teams have played 16 games each season since 1978. That could change. The NFL has considered making the season 18 games. After all, fans already watch the games in record numbers. But some people worry 18 is too many. The NFL season is already long. Plus, players might get injured more often.

Plus, it gives people plenty to talk about until the draft in May.

Free agency begins in the spring, too. That's when free agents can sign with new teams. These players have NFL experience. Sometimes they are superstars. This is an important time for any team. Adding the right players can turn a losing team into a winner. Teams also try to re-sign important free agents from their own team.

Next comes offseason practices. These are known as minicamps and organized team activities. Some of these events are just for rookies. They start learning the plays and getting used to their new team. Sometimes all of the players participate, though. These events give fans an idea of what to expect that season.

Then, in mid-July, training camp starts. All of the players report. They spend approximately three weeks together preparing for the preseason. The teams trim their squads down to 53 players over four preseason games. Then, in September, the season finally starts.

"What we have seen is that fans don't want [to stop following] football once the season is over," NFL commissioner Roger Goodell said. "They want more."

FUN FACTS AND STORIES

- NFL fans love a great debate. And one great debate took place before the 1998 NFL Draft. The Indianapolis Colts had the first pick. Many expected them to pick one of two quarterbacks. One was Ryan Leaf. He had been a star at Washington State University. The University of Tennessee's Peyton Manning was the other. The Colts ended up picking Manning. He went on to become one of the greatest quarterbacks ever. Meanwhile, Leaf was the second pick. But he struggled mightily and was out of the league by 2001.

- The NFL Network released its list of the league's top 100 players in 2014. The top 20 included five quarterbacks. That was more than any other position. The top six players on the list featured three quarterbacks. Denver Broncos quarterback Peyton Manning was number one. Tom Brady of the New England Patriots was third. Drew Brees of the New Orleans Saints was ranked sixth.

- In 1998, the St. Louis Rams finished with a 4–12 record. The following year, quarterback Trent Green suffered a season-ending injury in the preseason. A little-known quarterback named Kurt Warner became the Rams' starter. He went on to win the NFL MVP Award in 1999 while leading St. Louis to the Super Bowl title.

- Tom Brady was drafted by the New England Patriots in the sixth round of the 2000 draft. At minicamp later that summer, Brady approached Patriots owner Robert Kraft. He told Kraft, "We've never met, but I'm Tom Brady . . . and I'm the best decision this organization has ever made." Brady, of course, won three Super Bowl championships in his first four seasons as the team's starting quarterback. He added a fourth championship after the 2014 season.

GLOSSARY

agility
The ability to move quick and easily.

commissioner
An official in charge of an organization or league.

diehard
Strongly determined and devoted to a cause.

free agency
A portion of the offseason during which professional athletes without a contract are allowed to sign a new contract with any team.

intimidating
Frightening or scary.

re-sign
To agree to a new contract with a player who was already a member of the team.

rivalry
Competition that is particularly fierce.

rookie
A first-year player.

scouting
Observing in search of gaining information or knowledge.

skill position
Players who regularly touch the ball, namely running backs and wide receivers.

tailgating
Partaking in a social gathering that often takes place around a parked vehicle, typically in the parking lot of a stadium.

upset
An unexpected result or outcome, particularly in sports.

FOR MORE INFORMATION

Books

Frederick, Shane. *Side-by-Side Football Stars: Comparing Pro Football's Greatest Players*. North Mankato, MN: Capstone Press, 2015.

Rausch, David. *National Football League*. Minneapolis, MN: Bellwether Media, 2014.

Wilner, Barry. *The Super Bowl*. Minneapolis, MN: Abdo Publishing, 2013.

Websites

NFL Rush
www.nflrush.com

Pro Football Hall of Fame
www.profootballhof.com

Pro Football Reference
www.pro-football-reference.com

Sports Illustrated Kids
www.sikids.com

INDEX

About the Author

Drew Silverman is a sportswriter based in Philadelphia. He graduated from Syracuse University and has worked for ESPN, Comcast SportsNet, and NBC Sports. He also was sports editor of *The Bulletin* newspaper in Philadelphia. He lives in Philadelphia with his wife and his son.

READ MORE FROM 12-STORY LIBRARY

Every 12-Story Library book is available in many formats, including Amazon Kindle and Apple iBooks. For more information, visit your device's store or 12StoryLibrary.com.